MORE PRAISE FOR
BEAST AT EVERY THRESHOLD

"Natalie Wee's inventiveness in *Beast at Every Threshold* queers the reader's expectations with gravity and delight—the readings and misreadings cause an alignment of psychic, natural, worldly, and political precarities balanced in the speaker's body."

—RAJIV MOHABIR, AUTHOR OF *CUTLISH* AND
ANTIMAN: A HYBRID MEMOIR

"Through imaginative and dexterous forms, Natalie Wee invites the reader to stand face-to-face with language. Yes, language has a body, and it is evident in these poems, which tenderly dress the wounds from history, longing, and 'the world we must pass through to arrive at ourselves.'"

—HIEU MINH NGUYEN, AUTHOR OF *NOT HERE*

"Natalie Wee's searing lyric accesses an embodied record where shards of language reveal fractures made by repeating generational violence. Wee becomes a portal between worlds, teeming with polyphonic utterances ... that pulse through the sinews of the queered immigrant body."

—VANESSA ANGÉLICA VILLARREAL, AUTHOR OF *BEAST MERIDIAN*

"*Beast at Every Threshold* is electric with the possibilities of reading. As queer desire might abide beside loss, Natalie Wee refracts resistance and love through pop culture to formal influences, encountering the grief of surviving and witnessing 'after the fact.'"

—YANYI, AUTHOR OF *THE YEAR OF BLUE WATER*

BEAST

AT

EVERY

THRESHOLD

POEMS

NATALIE WEE

ARSENAL PULP PRESS
VANCOUVER

BEAST AT EVERY THRESHOLD
Copyright © 2022 by Natalie Wee

SECOND PRINTING: 2023

ARSENAL PULP PRESS
Suite 202 – 211 East Georgia St.
Vancouver, BC V6A 1Z6
Canada
arsenalpulp.com

The publisher gratefully acknowledges the support of the Canada Council for the Arts and the British Columbia Arts Council for its publishing program, and the Government of Canada, and the Government of British Columbia (through the Book Publishing Tax Credit Program), for its publishing activities.

Arsenal Pulp Press acknowledges the xʷməθkʷəy̓əm (Musqueam), Sḵwx̱wú7mesh (Squamish), and səl̓ilwəta?ɬ (Tsleil-Waututh) Nations, custodians of the traditional, ancestral, and unceded territories where our office is located. We pay respect to their histories, traditions, and continuous living cultures and commit to accountability, respectful relations, and friendship.

Cover artwork and design by Mia LaPine (Litarnes)
Text design by Jazmin Welch
Edited by Jasmine Gui
Proofread by Alison Strobel

Printed and bound in Canada

Library and Archives Canada Cataloguing in Publication:
Title: Beast at every threshold : poems / Natalie Wee.
Names: Wee, Natalie, author.
Identifiers: Canadiana (print) 20210388595 | Canadiana (ebook) 20210388609 |
    ISBN 9781551528830 (softcover) | ISBN 9781551528847 (HTML)
Subjects: LCGFT: Poetry.
Classification: LCC PR9570.S53 W443 2022 | DDC 821/.92—dc23

Even flying
is born
out of nothing.

—LI-YOUNG LEE

Any adjective can be true
if you cry hard enough.

—HIEU MINH NGUYEN

CONTENTS

HOLD

IN DEFENCE OF MY ROOMMATE'S DOG

humping her stuffed bear all day, even when guests laugh & turn their eyes

to a ceiling that will never demand the ugliest lie they've practised in the name

of survival. A decade ago, I watched my classmate open a doorway beneath the desk

because she wanted escape & thought to summon one with desolate, shaking fingers.

I don't know if I'm real when I'm not being touched: the loneliest prayer

of any small god. *Humiliate* translated: 丢脸, to lose face. Once, I lost myself

& found an instrument of forgetting, let someone's lover fashion from the ocean

of my solitude a shoreline for their sins to wash up on. Yes, I was an animal

crafting fables in the language of my body's flood. It's amazing what a little death

earns you. We imagine a funeral each time we peel back fresh need: *wait for me,*

it's cold, I'm scared. Maybe the trade-off for resurrection is shame vast enough to kill

us & that becomes another execution to tongue our way out of. Look. Here are primal

& ungainly ways we tether ourselves to the earth. Here is this dog fucking something

she imagines loves her, tiny heart thundering towards some vast & unknowable

glory, in the name of not vanishing just a little longer.

THRESH

RINA SAWAYAMA SINGS "I WANNA BE WHERE YOU ARE"

through the speakers / the lovers' lips blade-thin / as if whittling their faces /
to an echo / is to understand / the thing itself / how a voice can be slick rainfall /
poured over a metal carcass / it's no surprise / machinery betrays them /
everyone finds ways / to leave / decades later a child takes a plane / a man takes
a mistress / but in 1981 a Datsun slinks past the city / where dogs slobbered /
by the makeshift stadium / & a single word / whistled through enough teeth /
became legend / snap of jaws / in the blue evenings / already vanishing /
as they beg / hands from the hours / she licks ravenous decades / from her gums /
& tongues chill air into cavity / awaiting the tow truck / to deliver them / whole
as newborns / to shiver beneath / a motel's naked bulb / here / an ode
to failure / so simple / it allowed them this / tender mercy of staying *close* / *enough*
to feel / *your pulse baby* / what is the name / for where the chorus
splits / the star-dappled mangroves / & highways thronged
with mountains / harvested first-hand / from ink
-wet pages / the universe poetic / of course / she made this up /
adorned this recollection / with the boy's sprawl / on the hood / instead of his palm /
at the wheel / all urgent faux leather / tunnelling through wind / the day
steeped in language / only the body speaks / years breaking bone
-bright / over their eyes / as the radio shivers / into static / yes she knows /
every song / idols its own end

INSIDE JOKE

about that time w/ the cat & can of tuna which ended w/ me meowing up a tree

did u know cats learned 2 meow by imitating the cry of a human child
    each sound an imperfect, tender concession

we meow back: ouroboros

we meow back: Wiki says it's mirroring: we echo what we love
2 keep it

I love it when I text A & J "usual tn?" & we all reach Rol San for dim sum at 7

my bb sends a pic of 2 otters + the word "us"

translated: we exist in every iteration of touch made possible

yk there's a science 2 the sequence of butterfly emoji + rocket emoji + flamingo emoji

a pic of Patrick Star shovelling dirt in his mouth can mean
                  I'm upset right now or *attention please*

understanding memes is a kind of alchemy imho

after finals we'd toss our textbooks & scream *no more mugging!*

ma was mugged on Adelaide, S sobbed that Toronto winter

depending on who's talking, a sound/image/action has infinite lives

fuck language purists, *goodbye* only exists bc sum1 wrote *god*
    be with ye in shorthand

BTS said there's a whale that speaks only to itself, born w/ everything it knows
already in its blood

every instance I wrote 2 reach u thru this page
is its own kind of holy

tbh, we are so damn lucky to be loved like this
    w/ endless ways 2 bless one another

    our voices crowned w/ something new

                    & tender

        & no one else's

BORDERSONG

On a hostile beach,   eyes fixed
on glimmering edges   of an old world, you
were already forgetting   your real name. Not the one
borne from parents' care   .   ful knowledge of glamour
ous silver screens & all-   american sweethearts, each
syllable leashing your neck   in preparation for years
of saddling new tongues   to waiting throats.
No, not that. The one once given   by a fortune teller
who saw a distant horizon burn   ing to silence.
The birth name that means   iridescent. Means
radiant puncture seen only   in the absence of white
light. But hush. Be a pet   that stays soft. Be
careful   to call yourself   lucky. Open your eyes,
girl. No one looks   like you. Only wants
wear your warm skin   for sleek exotic fur,
stalk the place   you were born   & own it.
You stand   on so many graves
built out of any   one a little too
foreign. The invisible collar   you call flesh.
Try not to be   wound. No grievances.
Perfect accent. Always   laugh. Learn
how many reinventions   it takes to become
someone other   than dirty ungrateful   [   ]
when you are always already   Other

"CAN YOU SPEAK ENGLISH?"

Beached animals know sand
will smother any open maw

& an object in motion knows the ground.

We were shored clean of fathers,
throated harsh american accents
& muzzled breathing, only to be offered
a name half-pronounced. *Haunting*,

the border agent called me, instead of *Huan Ting*.
A single exhale dislocating phantom from girl. At the next
checkpoint, fluorescent menaces Mama's dark hair.
The long vowel of incoming headlights.

She fumbles, the stutter of birthing an unwelcome
child to a violent nation that does not know it—
each lonely syllable a stillborn. A precious age
bent before capricious white guards, praying

for a shadow that wouldn't break when held captive
to where the sun sets. Even before the ocean's
edge, sediment was mama's first Caesarean:
monuments planted by men who came, saw

& cast away. So she knifed a belly made for
easier spoils, sewed her tongue backwards.
Until she could not drink but held clay behind teeth
for daughters to build stairways out of.

Until they took to walking & forgot flight.
How a mother tongue becomes that
which she guards alone. How its usurper, birthed
from an arrow's eye, invents absence via arrival—

how this rotten tooth festers & demands
to be spat—how both a well-aimed question

& any apparatus of torture require satisfaction
to cease their patient cutting. & now I wear my
mother's skull, sour the native tongue with seethe.

You, Haunting. Where are you from?

& salt propheting a cemetery of stones,
my pockets weighed with beach.

FIELD NOTES: TIME TRAVEL

a name is only lyric

until we know what it commands

carp spiral upstream   stars embroider their shapes

to unknowable rhythms   in heavenly streets

birds in formation

water races what it carries   unfold an arrow   gravity turns our futures

so the sky never escapes   here—on this page   on an invisible spit

for the root of *fathom*   for language, like all things invented

is the length of outstretched arms   on Earth, is fashioned from it

the only difference between a dream & shadow

is the body light passes through

ASAMI WRITES TO KORRA FOR THREE YEARS

That night thickened with summer, beneath a bridge
illuminated by gold-trimmed lanterns, we blurred the pond
    with watching.

You told me about the dream in which you were the last bird
in the world, born an elegy to flight, how you woke grieving
the animal you could have been
        with the ferocity of the sky's gaping mouth,

        enjoyed the moment you had no one left
to disappoint before remembering why. My love,
               what we make of loss is a sport
    that kills.

Your daily return to the knifepoint of a burning city,
planting loyal bones in the earth
    to beg for those faces the soil now mothers.

Despite the birds nearly gone, the falling of other things
to the earth so slowly we could almost
        find above each growing shadow
    a wing shaped from fire.

The soft body that bore you across any distance wept

I wish the earth only moved when I let it.

My life, standing still despite this fact

is, too, an act of defiance.

It is not the moon's light that demands our praise

but the space it travels

to reach us.

AN ABRIDGED HISTORY

Every sentence I start about a man who hurts me ends
with the sentence about the men who hurt my grandmother.

I peer through this bloodline & find on the other end
a man wearing a bullet for a face, convinced a girl

is the width of his fist. Beyond her breath I step through
the door singed open & four women pressed to the dirt floor

of an attap house, uniformed beasts tugging the shell of an ear
just visible behind close-cropped hair, mud-streaked nails

bruising the delicate indent once left by an earring,
asking: *Nán? Nǚ?* in Mandarin learned from a military officer

who first taught them the words for *surrender* & *siege*.
Her sisters, looking not at the soldiers' faces but their fists

then all at once lunging. How it looked to a child hidden
under the bed's slender frame: four bodies vanishing

& then appearing through the window, a cluster of sparrows
rising into the season's heat. The pause between their leaving

& resurrection sharpened into a song about survival.
How she first clutched this prayer beneath the heavy tree

with the neighbour boy & his fangs, then every evening
at the gambler's feet as he conjured escape

through the neck of a bottle & later his wife. Each memory
fractures into the gesture from which her daughters rose

& then her daughters' daughters: how to hold close
the precious certainty of violence with an end.

Every fact I know unravels into this testimony.
It will never be over because it was told in the softest

part of her bones, passed through the velvet marrow
that lies within my body. It means that when

I return uncorpsed & say *Ahma, a man hurt me*
she says *it's over, bǎobèi,* & looks

beyond the bruises mottling my neck
to the breath in my mouth.

SKIN HUNGER, WITH WAVES

According to marine biologists
    we can map the migration of whales
by patterns in their songs, each lullaby
cued to a blueprint

                    of yesteryear.
When the horizon thinned to a thread
we stitched our voices to phone lines
& wove a soundscape of salt mist.

      I told you about the beach
covered entirely in boulders,
deepening faces carved from dusk.
    The path terraformed by waves

hauling the heaviest parts of itself
onto the shore, sea creatures
    writhing beneath my toes
starved with the same failures
of memory.

         This sentence,
like all others, reaching for you
out of metaphor.

I tried to build a pain
-less home & thought I failed
because I only had my body.

But your sharp kiss was a promise
I failed because the body is a question
                   only touch can answer.

Flanked by wild birds
          on rust-coloured sand
          I too was an animal
tamed by bewildering grace.

          Every place our skin touched
was a chord of perpetual radiance,
pure sound
               moving through the night.

We lay there as the world darkened, listening
          until mosquitoes fell upon us large & greedy
hungry for something good of their own.

BLOOD TRIPTYCH

You're twelve when papa says *it's not incurable*.

Just like that. Your tongue
smeared with blood

rich stew. That evening
a howl pierced you

in the longest fraction
of severed day: your face

a grey period to the whisper
between wood & frame

you watched a woman
flatten her palms

into a sheet thin enough
to pass through.

Let it be quick, mama begged,

& you didn't know then
she meant doctors' scalpels,

the razor's insistent kiss.

Her face in prayer was smoothed by darkness

into a shadow
curdled beneath the family

portrait. Now, Mama
lifts a thick cut

of sweet & sour pork
from her bowl to yours,

spoils silence with its fall.
Listen: eat: this meat

was once the softest part
of prey

pinned beneath a knife.

Because pets are counterfeit enough
to prepare children for grief

                    you invent birds with an absence
                    to survive after. To survive

every funeral, you rinse your eyes
with incense & practise flight

                    by wolfing your bones whole,
                    ready for the executioner

that stalks your lineage & births
hunt from hunger. In his last weeks

                    after chemo, your grandfather
                    breakfasts from his wife's urn,

measures devotion in swallows
of ash. Sickness feasts our meat until

                    we are wild enough to root in.
                    The consequence of rib

is cage.

a man bent double

gravity a shroud

& scarlet summons

speak softly

so not to wake

whatever unravels

forked red rivers

our truest sovereign

sickness an inheritance

to end

at the heels of

the limbs obedient

to blood's command

with his bones

fevered hollow

a man you love

mutinies the scalpel

its ceaseless work

& scripted gutting

from your pulse

carve a firebird

scorch the hospital

into ruined ark

garland your father

with the volta

where a surgery gown

thrown into air

shrinks into painless nimbus

& death has a face

into which you pool fury

miniature tornado　　　necessary violence

something to touch

instead of something

touching you

FREQUENT FLYER PROGRAM

I can name any season, but the trees I love will die

where they are. That's what it means to become a light

year, to become memory: never stay long enough
to speak belonging the way ocean pronounces the sky,

the world's translucent lung—the deadliest mammal
quietest. The hospital says I was conceived

as va███████de by being cut out of a woman,
& just like that she was proof I once stayed

long enough to be born.

When the airplane rattles I pray

grandmother in every language I know
to keep gravity from splintering my bones.

I call her *beloved*, sayang, saying
to myself, isn't my mother's tongue

the only thing they can't make me surrender
at the border?   Say diaspora.   Say destroy

                    that sickness & stay
                    a good wife. Say destroy

the old grudge & stay
a good citizen. Say

emigrate.   Say ingrate.

It's not too late to turn back if I can crush

       every doorway I've passed through to a story—
even in this dream of a house without papers.

       Everything built from ichor & sheet
music. I ask the sliver beneath passages

       to reveal someplace I can mistake for light.

I ask new anthems to greet me with a jaw

       soft enough to hold my name.

BECAUSE "SAN JUNIPERO" SAID
THE QUEER BAR IS A MARRIAGE HALL

you swore   the fluent in dying   but not yet dead

speak the language of touch   to make sure

the club haven   for what the day miscarries

how certain hungers blossom   only in the dark entered

through a lover's wet sigh   this ache an electric prophecy

we still have bodies   to call our own

& what a word   *ours*   nectar-sweet & next to oh

yes what further proof   holy is a song   whole as hunger

slick your hair with two fingers' worth of joy

put on a laugh that outruns   your last apology

& blow a kiss to each mirror's darling

we were promised at least   this rain   bow of sparks

music that dazzles the ear's whorl   a grace we can bear to live in

c'mon   faster please   shimmy so smooth

we sidestep our worst mistakes   chin up now

I won't beg   but believe me when I say

tomorrow's on the way & she's a stunner

here's the processional   the major key

applause all around   for the deities

we step into   to wife the space

between hip & heaven   praise this sweat-bright nape

taut with new rapture

love, let us live   if just for tonight

in one another   & reinvent the beast

with two backs   one to shoulder our names

the other to riot   a new temple

in which we come over & over

into ourselves

gorgeous   deathless   free

worshipped by true believers

on bent & patient knees

MUSIC THEORY: OPUS

When someone asks, *what are you doing*, & you say
my best, all wry voice & twisted mouth, I remember:
before I was a mother, I was a child
that heard Chopin in passing. The polished blue bicycle
zipping by the roadside stall where we crowded six to a table
& waited. In what seemed like hours but spanned mere seconds
it took for lap cheong to sizzle garlic into sensational flavour
that fragment of sound from the gleaming transistor radio
was our only sustenance. I didn't know what I had heard,
only that my life had expanded around the shape
of this gift. At the school's broken-down piano
I would trace the path of what I recalled
until I reached the threshold of what lay after.
Each note, lifted from the ruins of memory,
was dusted free of rubble, then tested against the skeleton
of an unknown beast. Again, until its limbs moved
the way it needed to, the way I thought it could,
until it outran my callused fingers. Decades later
your friend asks, over FaceTime, *what are you doing?*
On the court, strapping teenagers watch a boy try
& fail to deliver the basketball into the hoop's patient embrace.
No matter: back slaps all around. They understand risk.
Chin up, his elders say, as he strains for the next shot.
You understand, don't you, when you answer,
my best. Yes, I remember this: the first time I listened

to a tape of my favourite ghost. You, half-asleep & suckling
at my breast. The gravity of knowing that filled me
as I filled you.

SELF-PORTRAIT AS MONSTER DATING SIM

How long have you been around?

Long enough to split the first echo.

Do you remember what you looked like?

What do you think you look like now?

A thumbprint of dew.

A moon without a sky to hold it in.

Do you pray?

What scares you the most?

To the clock's pendulum.

The dark.

What do you pray for?

Is that the truth?

The shape of your future feels like rain you've touched only in the dark.

Do you love the night?

What else will save me?

What keeps the body from other bodies?

You want to know if you're safe.

All I have are these hands.

What will save me then?

Loneliness.

Whose loneliness?

And how long have you been lonely?

COPING MECHANISMS

i am young & want to leave

i touch myself all day,
broth marrow & salt.

it's a fact orgasm is closest
to death without dying.

like any brute i cannibal my flesh

feet first, cleave an archway
to walk through & name it

a bruise of family albums.

a man turns into a rusted gate

a wife gardens her blood,
ribbons tree rings for years.

her ankles sprout two birds,
instruments of wind & song

to hunt what lies out of reach

like a field of stars in a photograph
i once tried to hold without creasing

the radiance inside. ask: i

name a woman & a daughter   will answer: the mother of my mother
                                   lived by bent knee & bleach, foretold

                                   bedrooms blazed into museums of
                                   yellowed light. When i was born a moon

split the sky with hot yolk   prophesied a season of waste

a mother swollen with weeping & years   i know. i know my mother

could not leave   because i arrived

IN MY NEXT LIFE AS A FRUIT TREE

which by all accounts is a foolish aspiration
considering deforestation rates & forest fires.
    If there is a choice, why not be the pangolin that wades
through a mangrove whispering gnats? Why not the wind
    chime overlooking an occupied birdhouse? Or the spoon
nestled in a parent's fresh-made broth, or the signal
    emitted by a distant star that'll touch the earth only once
but it's clear, isn't it, how these are infinite mirrors
    everything chrysalis, relentless

            & becoming, & watch me become
bedrock, root of the root, wild & wildling.
    Who knows which sweet burden my tree will bear,
jambu ayer or starfruit or mandarin orange
    but I'll flower one crop each day for as long
as the palm reaching upwards needs something to adore it
    & there is, for one moment, relief because I am
& am enough. So forget theories of sorrow
    & hellfire & brimstone at the final circle of the earth:
if I must believe in anything, I choose this: my lover
    whispering, *in my next life, I want to be*

            the bird that rests on your branches—
knowing the whole while

        in my next life, I want to be
is already a complete sentence.

TEN YEARS AFTER DIAGNOSIS

A river carves its grief
into soil
        & we have a valley.

A moon pours itself
over creation myth
        & we have a woman.

A child believes the story about Van Gogh
& yellow paint. Bent over the toilet, she reels light
from herself.
      Against porcelain, gold dust swirls like clouds
brined with stars. Her face a crescent moon.

In geology, *depression* is a type
of landform. The etymology   of this condition: the Latin word
        for *press down.*

Despite the risk of arteries compromised by nitrogen or lungs shattered with deadly force, a seafarer once braved watery corridors to name the yoke of tectonic plates an oceanic trench. Therefore the gullet of the world, so deep it lay unknown to the sun, was touched at least once.

A brief list of wants: the lacquered sun,
the neighbour's dog & its downy fur, love
    spilled over a garish purple sofa like fruit
hurtling from trees.

    To own the word *I*, to sink
      your teeth into its meat,   how even its shape resembles a bone
          to suck the pith of life from.

    This body isn't a trial run
    for your real life.
        Take your life

    in your hands. Make your hands useful
    or you'll be sorry.
        You say sorry

more than anything else.

Another urban legend: animals will abandon offspring
touched by human beings. This, too, has been disproven
by wildlife experts, although it is easy to believe

                        our hands are capable of so much
hurt.

Wildflowers by the hospital window sit in their skin, resplendent,
giving their future selves over to time, failing to do anything else
but exist. Sure, the gardener comes. The dog comes.
A well-intentioned child with a magpie's sensibility comes.
Still, they rise from the dirt, beholden to & envious
of no one, convinced none of this means they don't deserve
to be loved.

IN THE MOOD FOR LOVE

Bed traced with smoke, you circled my palm's horizon

       said, *that's your heart line* & I learned greed

             can engineer a kingdom

out of any wreckage. I imagine you've lain this way

    with your lover, your bodies

        a wingspan apart as they marvelled

            at the gorgeous dip

        in your cheek, obliging North Star

to greedy fingers framed by your face.

    Your breath lullabies my veins with absence, the gulf

        between us bridged by dawn

      broken through legs of mothers we left behind.

When I tell you about the greenhouse

    scorched to memory

      I mean I understand

        the phrase *to carry a torch,* this ache

that sparks each time I pronounce your lover's name.

How, in place of your pliant lips

I seek out the precise shard

    of light blazing over your smooth cheek.

O tender thorn, O most beautiful

    splinter, O sweet bruise

        O my fleeting joy upon this Earth

    praise your careless shimmy

as you flower pink mornings

    via cast iron pan & stove.

    Praise a tongue so wondrous

        you pronounced my longing

            a day kind enough to sleep through.

Praise the wingbeat of your eyelashes,

    the steady of your voice

        as you forgive my pulse & its treason.

        Praise your wide-shouldered slouch

ferrying through the dark

as you go home

    to someone else who loves you.

SELF-PORTRAIT AS POP CULTURE REFERENCE

I was born in 1993, the year Regie Cabico became the first
Asian American to win the Nuyorican Poets Cafe Grand Slam.

I want these facts to mean something to each other
the way a room is just a room until love or its inverse

tells me what to do with the person standing in it.
Once, I stood on a street corner & a white woman, stunned

by the horizon I passed through to be here, put her paws
on my face to relearn history. I was named after a movie star

who died by drowning, *A Streetcar Named Desire* gone now
to brine, & split the sea every year to see my mother again.

The first man I loved named me after a dead American
& crushed childhood into a flock of apologies.

The women I loved taught me that water cures anything
that ails, given enough thirst. I speak thirst,

sharpen the tongue that slithered through continents
& taught my ancestors to pray its name. I pray its name

& so undertake the undertaker, it preys my Mandarin name
so I watch Chinese dramas with bright-eyed bodies

to forestall forgetting my own. I've watched my skin
turned fragrant ornament thrown over women

the colour of surrender & they were praised for wearing it.
I wake wearing my skin & praise myself for waking.

My skin, this well-worn hide I fold into a boat
sturdy enough to bisect any body of water

was made from light breaking over my mother's face—
my mother lifting her fingers to the sky & inventing

the where she touched & swallowed it whole.
I've swallowed every name I was given

to spit them back better. To write is to cradle myth
& memory both & emerge with the fact

of your flesh. I praise the first book
that touched me because it was beautiful,

because it was written by a stranger born looking
just a little like me & that made him beautiful, & in it

I find every person I've loved into godhood
tunnelling through the page & beyond the echo

of those precious trees allowing breath: their shadows
blurring into a wave, rich & urgent, to greet me.

BIRTHRIGHT

Of all my inheritances   the ancestral appetite

pulls heaviest   the translucent ache   licks my joints sweet   a hound

without a muzzle   begging not   for fullness   but to be rid

of absence   a man who praises   the water's return to shore

transforms my leaving   into his life's end   foretells a child

made sinew & weight   made a lifetime   of burials   have you watched

sun-dappled foam   grow molars & shatter   over jagged stones

filthiest canines   multiplying what it's fed   to keep eating

we are born into   an economy of desire   & belly ancestral wants

to marrow our bones   & furnish bodies   with our blood's   basest greed

what is permanence   if not a fiction of mercy   what is a name

to slice from the day's   golden hour   if not a lighthouse

if I could eat my lonely   *if I could fluent my lonely*

this slow heavy was both   my mouth   & its hollow   I mean hunger

hunger of a wave   cannibalizing itself   to reach shore   hunger

that folds inwards   because what else   will feed it

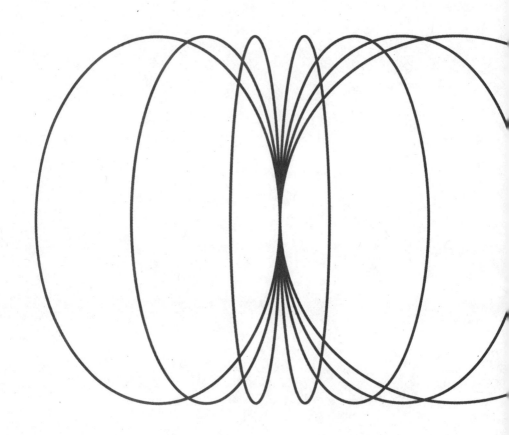

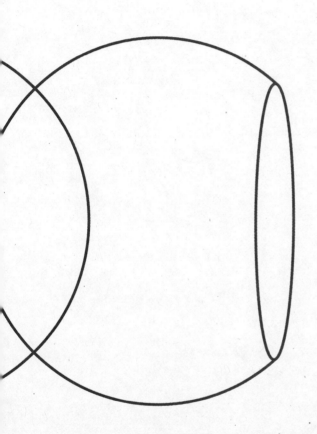

HOLD

WEI YING TELLS ME ABOUT RESURRECTION

I fell into a graveyard & crawled out a ghost. I was a relic of an age
no grace could touch, I slept in the underworld so I wouldn't look
at my fists. Daughter, you too reached the day through a blade
of light. In another life, you spend months bent over bins
doggedly chewing whatever kindness survives a stranger's hands
& the year prior kneeling before a boy who knows the rift
between a life measured in government paper & disappearing
is how quietly you scream inside the smallest hour. We own nothing
but our ends. I am no prophet, but know this: any devil
worth their salt swears fealty to blood alone,
knowing hurt, like any animal, lives only to bury itself
in the heat of its truest grief. In place of my human face
I stride into a veil of killing season. Because I was a bride
to violence, I kissed every crime I could name & smithed a halo
of their architects. Anything can be a weapon in the right clutch.
When a man next raises his fist, unhinge your jaw & retch
the knife that skeletons you. Child, be ruthless. Be cut
throat. In all of eternity, you learn there is no forgiveness
to be crowned with. A joke I was once told goes, *I didn't choose
this life, this life chose me*. Fuck that. Choose a hell
of your own making over the hell that unmakes you. Flower
a garden of rage & eat & eat & eat.

INSTRUCTIONS FOR A TRANSMUTATION CIRCLE

Kite a red arrow above the dragon-
          fly nets & mimosa field,
god gathers her tools. Twine in her palm
glows with leftover condensation
from the abandoned carton of chrysanthemum tea
    where a straw bends in sugar,
a branch reaching through the season
Mama realized everything would change.
She craved what the girl held fast, like a newborn:
       possibility, or the world opening
to a hall of indeterminate shape.
What must she carry? She was told everything
is allegory: aphid-heavy foliage & lusty flowers,
fat koels naming themselves
     to cicada applause, the mud-smeared sign
         before an enclaved sapling that announces
    I'm on my way, do not kill me! all reminders
that tomorrow is the sole fiction geography allows.
If she let it, tomorrow can begin
         with go. Go ahead. Go home. Go
    on, good, we're good, my love, we're safe
now. & now god's bent head ascends, a familiar eclipse
of furred brow & sun-warm sweat.
Her mouth a door, after which
       there is another door.

IMMIGRANT AUBADE

I knew you first as the shape of some bird
& then the warble that quickens air into spring.

My throat overflows with the lullaby
of we who name our motherlands

the place where sunset meets the sea,
we for whom maps hold no wonder

our bodies can't outmatch. It's magic, how
another diasporic darling makes

where are you from sound like sisterhood
instead of a reminder I'm not really *from here.*

Here, where someone's dreams brought us.
The centuries gave us each other & then

the word *we*: the small mercies of those
who soften days into instant Maggi on blue ceramic,

hum my grandmother's favourite song
& peel the spiderwebbed shell of boiled eggs

the way one would pluck the bluest fish scale
      from a child's mouth, delicately, with fingers

that refuse stillness & silence.
    We who belong to ourselves in any city.

              We of elsewhere & I'll keep you safe.
        We a people of longing & children of belief.

      When asked *where are you from* again
we answer with someplace

          named after each other.

PHONING HOME TO TELL MY GRANDMOTHER
I SURVIVED A HATE CRIME

Ahma, 亲爱的 / 您好吗? / my beloved / my life's great joy / yes, something
happened / of course you can tell / by my voice / who was it that said / the body
is the sound / hurt makes / that we were born / a prelude to cleave / Ahma /
您听到吗 / a white woman / mistaking me / for animal / feeling behind / my teeth /
for our country / discovering only / my mother tongue / some thief's trick / cheap
as yellow / skin spits warning / a war cry / I remember / back then / how you robed
yourself / in tall grass / how your waiting / shrunk soldiers' bayonets /
into a single hairpin / muzzling the sun's eye / you watched them / mount the earth /
all monsoon / & thought / even light begins / & ends somewhere / what more
a nation / what more a citizen / I am not / a citizen / crossed all
that water / just to live like a dog / I thought of you / 亲爱的 /
as this undertaker / warmed her grandfather's fists / on Mama's face / in mine /
planted her foot / where another golden daughter / could someday rise /
called herself a fierce / & terrible god / & she was/is a god / of this city / this land /
where our colour / is fresh meat / new leather / good leash / Ahma / 别哭了 / my love
I know / all that distance / & my name through it / is the sound of / breathing
in reverse / the audacity of being here / the audacity of being / here /
you taught me / the mandarin word / *to bear* / 忍 / is written knife / over heart /
& the sound of hurt / ends at the close / of my life

ASAMI WATCHES KORRA IN THE REAR-VIEW

The dead rise between our teeth in the aftermath
of another feast, phantom ruminants marching
through the underworld with wine-dark hooves.

How often we've slit through an animal or man
to keep ourselves whole. But for you, love,
I have freed myself of gauntlets. I am gaunt

with tonguing your name this shy of bruise, each syllable
a measure of how long I have watched a boy
to find the girl he was looking at, adored only a reflection

which demands nothing for the price of sight.
If the greatest measure of devotion is to hunger
without bite, let looking be a placeholder for a kinder want.

Praise the miracle of glass that allowed me to touch you
before I ever touched you, telegraphed your palm's heat
& its nearness to dawn, assured me the heave of your chest

chases a precious pulse that holds back death & its chariot.
Praise the spell for the woman drenched with moonbeam
laughing in the back seat of my father's red automobile,

the slope of your neck as you shriek birds into the cool dawn.
Praise the marvel of a love I have yet to bury.
Praise the miracle of your dark hair. Your fingers tightening

around the leather armrest as we tunnel through bright & wind.
Your eyes catching in the glass like headlights. The safety label
swearing subjects in the mirror are closer than they seem.

INTERRUPTION: B-SIDE

here's the man who swears to die unless we love him forever

&

the girl who survives that violence	violence that survives the girl who
becomes flood the cleanest cut	becomes boat a slender scab
the day's split lip a man	the land's loose tooth a man
feeding the lake his knees	his head full of lit matches
her spine his hands	her throat his hands
does it matter if the tide never	does it matter if the hull brooks
comes sharpened if hurt carves	only leaving if escape paths
itself in something's bones	its way through injury

a moon   a mirror   a girl

what is that parable about stones	what is that parable about sieves
& a jar of water she draws	& warm places she dresses
trench into pool brief spill	house into window little knife
maybe a daughter is just a breath	maybe a daughter is just a breach
to soften burial into bed	made flesh to rupture

maybe a name is just what

makes her knowable in the dark
so say father   or forgiveness
say that cool rush thickening north
is grief's true cartography
hurt   ling at the speed of girlhood
this too is a country   to live
in   this umbilical slit
blunts the rock   enough to hold it
loves the man   enough to keep him

throttles heaven's waiting face
so say farther   or forgetting
say of the torque's swift whistle
every vessel was built elsewhere
hurt   ing at the speed of absence
this too is a country   to leave
behind   this lightning-sheer sail
cleaves the wind   enough to cross it
loves the shore   enough to look back

FAVOURITE TV TROPE

The umbrella sleeps
until it is needed, then remembered.
We know what this narrative demands: a vase broken
or saved from being broken, Polaroids of a life
before this one, debts owed or repaid. Call this
animal magnetism or a multitude of longings
to undo the self with. Who can claim
to know the invisible mechanisms
unfolding over all their lives—what object
requires no gratitude but weather
that hammers down like applause.
Little harbour which does its best work
when the scene opens with the clamour
of buses through an ankle-deep flood,
rivulets sprinting heavy over the windows.
This too is the law of natural things.
What glows between the drenched
 & once-drenched only looks simple,
a divinity made ordinary by practice.
All this has happened & will happen again:
someone stands on the curb, then stands over
a stranger who's spent the last hour mourning
the faces they discarded before deciding on this shape.
& the umbrella bends its head close, patient,
over the palm reaching through lashes of rain

as a new favourite voice says, like a storm
or the promise of one coming: *you exist to me*
& I'm going to let you.

SOMEONE IN SOME FUTURE TIME

Bare ankles track equatorial heat
across the fleeced sofa & a glossy television set coughs

into colour: *Alien* plasmas her room.
The girl's arm thrums sweat.

Her mouth constellates piano-crooked fingers
while you swell with sympathy for every starving beast.

Of course you know bellying need
that's impossible to kill—an invisible whelp

you'd do anything to jettison. This ache
of magnitude black hole. Instead you Kraken

a flotilla of spinal fluid & bioluminous hurt.
This desire is hyperintelligent,

craters itself in the membranes of flesh
while you pretend you've only been running

like everyone else, untouched & clean.

A mass of fevered limbs unwieldy with greed
thrash against the cavern of your diaphragm

& reassembles cartilage into a planet
habitable if only she'd come inside you

& stay, how you'd tail her orbit
　　　　as any celestial being obeys gravity—

do you know, you did not say, *how long*
　　　　eight years coalesces into a dim photograph

　　　　　　　　　　of one sweltering afternoon
　　when you looked at a beautiful girl & pretended

　　　　　　for one fleeting moment you were brave
　　　　　　　　enough to tell her just that

LISTEN I LOVE YOU JOY IS COMING

Despite a new death come to keep us from each other,
a constellation of birds sings outside your window

       & if you think their music thunderous,
how much more must it be for these creatures—
       but what do you know of why
they bleed noise?

       & what of the cry you make, soundless,
with each movement, from the soles of your feet
       to your finger thrust towards the sky,
another animal
       reaching for unnameable things

       it does not yet understand.

Scientists posit time moves differently for animals depending on size.

An island of birds sings
outside the window. Listen
they spend whole lives
mastering one kind of sorcery
& we love them not in spite
but because of this fact.

When you read this, are you passing through the speaker's time, or are they passing
through yours?

Despite a new death come to keep us from each other

hum while slicing carrots
& remember the night you first heard this song,
at the show with two of your dearest,
a handful of goldenrod in the crowd.

Months later a beautiful girl undressed
this rhythm from your skin
& fed it back as new movement,
rhythmic, like a knife
on a chopping board.

How much of the world must we pass through to arrive at ourselves?

One hundred days without touch
& the birds still sing: your voice still remembers
        its place: your hands still caress your flanks,
the bend of a knee, wiry pubic hair.

                    Praise that insistent text past midnight
                            & the incoming video call.
Look at you
        blowing pixelated kisses,
        roofing an aviary of gauzy postcards,

                offering gifts at front stoops
                awash with golden hour,
a houseplant or someone's favourite tea,
touch without touch,
                new ways to say

                the heart is the kindest homeland
        thank you
                skin can hold an archipelago of peace
        thank you
                there is so much joy this year
                hasn't stolen from us yet & I pray
                whatever that shines inside us bleeds

        gold   through & through & through

I ALWAYS BET ON LOSING DOGS

that one time the pub beneath us was on fire & she didn't make a sound,
not when opaque smoke climbed into our second-storey apartment like
a thundercloud over parched grass, not when the fire trucks pulled up
& my friend said, over the call punctuated by siren & enough heat to gnaw
through a cool March evening, *damn, what's that sorry excuse of a dog good for?*
But I understand. I too have cradled my loves to sleep in the arms
of a burning kingdom. I have kissed the ash of dreams & knelt before a door,
obedient, when a given name leashed me by the hair. Sure, she can't fetch,
can't roll over, can't stay, but every time we leave she transforms into a shrine
of longing—the truest weather. Who here hasn't launched themselves
at the slightest whisper in a house with no shadows? Who can deny
having tried to summon love from air with teeth alone? We return
& she muscles back from the dead, trembles until some god bestows the mercy
of a palm upon her head. After years of this it must be easy to mistake hell
for an empty room. As flames licked us out of the spit-slick hour
I imagine she curled in my lap, warm & finally satisfied, & thought to herself:
this is a dream clawed from every prayer made with my head to the ground, yes
this is as good a day as any to lay down & die.

SAYANG

Once, ▮▮▮ bent over my childhood bed,
his hands blooming a lake
the width of a girl's cheek warmed by summer.
I was hospital-blue & the soft membrane

between his knuckles were speckled with pinpricks
of white without them moving, this once. The quiet
inside them as they opened & shut, iterations
of every miracle possible before dusk. Now

▮▮▮'s voice, soft as if someone, somewhere, was asleep.
I'm sorry, he said. *You don't understand.*
It's like something takes over me. It's true.
It's true I learned the word for *strike* first-hand

& the backs of his palms were damp again.

+

Sayang (noun): dear, love

The bicycle tongues a plump hill, warmed by the weight of some daughter-shaped thing fresh from her ████'s steadying clutch. Months from rasped knee & shriek, decades still from becoming the echo of a single turn in deep sleep, there is a man at the bottom of this slope, at the end of my shadow. There is the field behind him, steeped with indigo-red fever. There are his arms holding the sky apart. He's grinning because there's no reason not to—because my life stretches before me & he's in it.

+

Once, ████ killed the world's smallest bird, which is why
Mama used to say a fuse was just the threat of too much light.
We have to keep it, he said, because it's hurt.
For two scant days it lay in a fish tank crosshaired

with thin wire, echo to the guppies, terrapin, & turtle
once adored & now somewhere after bone,
somewhere without eyes. Their bodies, each a gasp
& then gone. & as if it knew the dangers of hard love

the sparrow shredded hours for a sky just out of reach,
so afraid of becoming a name it was ready to die for it.
The shriek of an animal deboning itself for flight.
The shrill of living close enough to air to vanish.

I remember living inside that sound.

+

Sayang (verb): adore, love

Sheathing cards in a battered suitcase for discovery in hostels of faraway cities, each
aerogram bleeding COME BACK SOON ▇▇▇ in clumsy script, breaking our throats
on Michael Jackson's highest notes, belting my arms to a shrinking mango
tree, its scent thickening every room into plantation, despite the thin cane & its
sudden thrash, despite the bolted gate at midnight, despite Mama's soundless night
weeping, despite the shape of a grandmother hunched over me as a raised hand
makes thunder again.

+

Once, a ravenous thing sheared itself into
the shape of a boy, hungry despite broth steaming in
white-and-blue porcelain, clasped like a newborn
between two palms. He ducks for one moment beyond

his mother's noodle store & customer swelter, tips
the bowl's mouth to his lips in brief prayer
audible only to someone he has never touched.
He swears to become a boat bearing more than water

& to be a boat that always bears. & so becomes a man
who understands love only in measures of vessels,
nursing his children on the sweetest morsels of any meal
ferried back & forth kitchen islands:

you can have it. No, you. No, *you*.

+

Sayang (phrase): [it's] a pity

I wished myself into any season beyond the airport terminal & then watched my

█████ dissolve into just that. His hands, chilled by my hospital-stale cheek, shuttered

decades in a single wave—then returned once more to the suitcase filled with proof of

an old life. Again. His whole body, deft enough to rise into air, paused briefly at a

gate made of light. I didn't know whether to say goodbye or beg to be the telephone's

warble instead so I said, *thank you*

+

Once, a girl's blue shadow stretched through light years

of night terrors, thrummed into the shape of her █████'s arm

still tucked beneath her skull, slivered an arrow as she jolted awake—

█████? & his echo, *It's just a nightmare. Come back*

to sleep, into the dream with her █████ overlooking

a bed large enough for two children not yet caught in

the undertow of leaving. Four rabbit-soft breaths breaking

the stillness of a flat where no one he knew before

has been. Having already teethed a long bridge

to dry his limbs on the other side, bellied flags the colour

of a body emptying itself, he swears his young will never

need to swim. He swears on his only life that

everything they need is right where they stand.

EN ROUTE TO THE SIXTH STATION,
CHIHIRO COUNTS THE CLOUDS

suppose you make up your mind & certainty rattles like an empty train. astonishing
how almost everything involves blinking down at a ticket & deciding what to offer
in exchange for safe passage. we're all just passing through: a childhood passes
by, parents pass on, & what passes for rain in the city is a palm's worth of prophecy
with a 40% chance of error. we wake daily to the calendar's mundane wonder & think
nothing of the day's triumph, only of becoming someone for whom courage
is already fact. fact: a promise is an exercise of faith. paraphrased: destiny's
just a name for the next stop. we arrive at a kinder fiction by surrendering the self
to a new era. what must survive. what must survive us. an hour, a pendulum admits,
can last lifetimes, really, depending on how many you've lived. so perhaps alive at all
is alive enough. here's a mouthful of strawberries to sweeten the ride, a bouquet
of baby's breath to lay at every seat. here's a forgiveness we don't need to earn.
the cabin studded in Y2K pink & baby blue, a reel of someone's promised land
glittering through the windows. less a place, & more the year you thought
you'd never touch, kissing your cheeks at last.

AFTER THE ATLANTA SPA SHOOTINGS, WE SAT IN A FIELD

sprawled over grass

made an endless planet

by nightfall. Our faces

lifted to the season's end

were a cloister of moons.

I asked for a legend

about what glows

so we could fill our bellies

with something death

hasn't yet touched.

To be moved

by what's untouchable

means we are conduits for more

than flesh, fallibility.

To ready ourselves

for gentleness, then,

is to make a landscape

of desire, translate farewell

into the sum of all distances

measured by light.

Nothing's as visceral

as the hard-won kiss

where we press our lips

to ghosts & inhale

until we are vessels for life

still unlived.

Genealogy creates room.

I only have my shadow

to bear—& even that is theory

in another throat.

We are both endangered

species, you & I,

but the weight

of your heart's chambers

upon my breast

was a dream

no prayer could give us.

If there's anything

that still surprises me

it's the fact joy too has weight.

That at the end of all hurts

there lies another to climb out of

while wearing your own face.

SELF-PORTRAIT AS BEAST INDEX

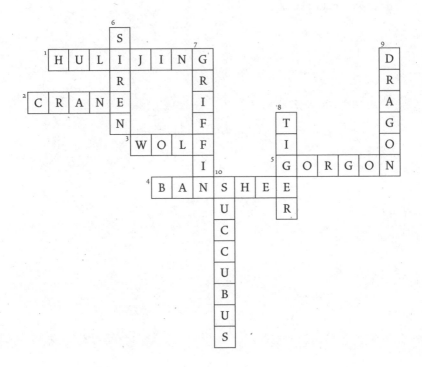

Across

1. when Ahma said we are born possessing infinite tears
   I thought she meant a bottomless spring
2. a vault of life we draw fervour from
3. but no, she meant *tiers*, as in, layers of soil to excavate
   before arriving at the mineral-rich loam
4. how each cry, barely audible, escapes the insect that made it
5. & claims its own absence to sate

Down

6. must draw from silence to decide its tenor
7. & sink into the ear's delicate archway, sparking neural sequences
8. that announce this is *song*
9. yes, we are woodwind whittled through with life
10. so speak to outlast the body

THAT TIME I THOUGHT PHOEBE BRIDGERS SANG, "WHEN I GROW UP, I'M GONNA LOOK UP FROM MY PHONE AND SEE MY WIFE"

& for the blissful minutes before I realize I misheard
  wife is a word borrowed from an altar not so different
from the one where I've smoothed my knees, making bargains
  with some higher power. There is a methodology
that begins with the spine in supplication, an offering made
  with upturned fingers & minted with breaths turned clouds.
The kind that thickens over the pool where a girl considers
  time & latitude, how to rinse off enough fear to emerge
a new fledgling, not knowing departure has a shape
  we pour ourselves into, or that there is an afterward
already fitted like a sheet around the last echo of our voices
  or what it means to love another woman & bury her
name under a tongue, to peel the sound layer by layer
  until each syllable becomes an eel's wafer-fin
that flounders in a throat—but reader, there is a time for that yet.
  First let us return to the scene with ya pears by the pool,
miniature suns swelling golden in the girl's chlorinated palm.
  As she licks the crisp tang from each wedge of light
she borrows from her future its sweetness, so ripe & full
  of yes, *life*—the one where she draws sugar from the lips of her lover
beneath a salt-humid evening flecked with scuttling crabs,
  a lover who murmurs, hey, *what's wrong? why are you crying?*

knocking sand-clotted sneakers against the pier's edge.

   & the girl, now grown, laughs, says *nothing*, says *my wife,*
my wife, I have everything I wanted.

WHEN MY GRANDMOTHER BEGINS TO FORGET

This sentence begins where her memory ends: my grandmother
           at dusk, calf-deep in water. The shoreline

    glittering amber bottles & footprints. Her palms
shatter the foam's pale roof, then emerge, clean & hollow.

        The simplest migration. No proof of motion besides
the unmistakable scent of salt. Now she looks, not at the water,

but the shine that bends through it. Dates or constellations,
      schooling just out of sight—names darting in unbridled spills.

      If she could only reach them, her sisters would return,
full-fleshed & gorgeous, & the unforgiving ache in her spine

      will unspool the weight of a child not yet born.
        Moons of her kneecaps scale the wet as she searches.

What she knows of loyalty is the unchanging horizon.
      Of keeping something safe in the throat without breathing.

        How she'd practised for months or years in that forest,
folded into the side of the attap hut, awaiting the warplane's

loose teeth, the soldiers spat out to speak the language of men.
She tells me because she cannot forget

& because she forgets she tells me again. Me, 宝贝
beyond the bayonet's bite in this story, because in her telling

I am not born until she remembers. & then I am born
as proof she survived. She survives whether or not I write this

after the fact. In a moment she will look up
& discover my body's reminder, fresh

from another airplane, but one sleeker & kinder. Her face split
not with the whistle of a far-flung boulder, the beggar's

bomb, but the sun breaking over us, a perfect Lunar
New Year's mandarin orange. *Ting-ah, look ...* beyond

waves flattening themselves against shoreline, gulls dive-bomb
foam into bloom. How gorgeous each radial shimmer,

testament to the daily attempt to outdo forces of nature.
How wonderful it is not to remember having failed.

FUTURE-PROOF

On the windowsill, the monstera launches skyward. In soil annexed by the glazed flowerpot, a cocktail of eggshells wink up like fallen petals, & what appears at first glance to be some caterpillar orgy reveals a tapestry of finely fuzzed vegetable peels. Salvaged from compost, survivors practise refuse of a different sort. Where they touch, the end is not the end. There is no rush. For weeks this precious rot softens with stores of minerals, the stink of nitrogen & sulphur a celebration of decay that nourishes the living. A shoulder's length away, basil & rosemary overlook the garbage truck which culls abandoned brethren, delivers rancid takeout to an unforgiving plant of steel & acid. In this home, where the veil between the mortal & underworld is porous, the monstera drinks. You've done your work, say the clefted leaves that brush the earth. Now let me do mine.

ETYMOLOGY OF MINOTAUR

Because even the body's rain

falls in coppered ellipses, I swallowed

      the feathers of every feral thing

   until I wombed a chimera, root of both idol

& monster. Not *pet*, meaning house

   -broken. Yes, a name can be the address

threading you to another portal

   as the sentence ends. Example: 疼: hurt:

the song in our bellies: a reminder: tenderness

      is the heart's revenge

   against bleed: what bleeds understands

hurt: 我疼你: I am tender for you. You slept

inside me for as long as I could bear

   before a dagger

      made you your own

   animal, found the place your skin ended

& tore it, a reminder

                    nothing awakens the flesh

like want. Child, I want you

                    to live. To live, I opened

        & retched until you were pure ink

& rapture. Your deathless pelt

                    nursed on the nipples

        of myth. My first bloodletting

                    came like a weapon

that did not know a body

        could hurt. You came

not like an answer

            but the mouth asking.

WHEN I SAY I WANT TO LEARN YOUR MOTHER'S RECIPE, I MEAN

Read three ways

ancient people shaped pots from clay

to make fire a thing to swallow

want & its answer prehistoric

our bodies fevers inherited from the earth

centuries of need forged from flesh

& gifted names

when you tongue my name

I understand how one mistakes the kind
-ling of lovers for a fuse / now that it's ended
/ now that skin is just skin & not

electricity that blesses touch

a summer of leftover longing

fizzes the air scorch-thick

flesh swelters into floodlight /

scientists say that energy

transforms into something else / desire

defies death itself / the window

blanched by every breath

between our mouths

witness to each humid dusk

thirst blisters /

like a kettle's keen whistle /
above a stove's helix coil

sweet now the flame's gone long & low

radiating the dream beneath my ribs

meat simmers & crisps

I AM MY DREAMING SELF GETTING BETTER AT THIS

Thesis: you are

therefore you carry

carry this body

season to season

carry your body

like glittering rainfall

in cupped palms

carry your body

like cresting prayer

to jewelled dawn

the dawn of

your body becoming

becoming soft

becoming a window

to look through

becoming wings

over the earth

the earth's gravity

bends you

        like rain

sculpting new colour

    for what it nourishes

like rain

     your veins buoyed

by summer

     one summer you sat

on a bridge shaking

    until the sun pierced

the landscape

     like god's arrow

through a doe mid-leap

    shaking your bones

free of another end

     shaking out

the grief of this name

     this name

your first language

     for *rise*

this name means be

        longing or forget

me not

             a name

to be known by

        arrives with heart

to bear

        so bear your ghost

-wreathed bloodline

          bear a shadow

burnished with waiting

              wait

your shadow is

        still your shadow

your shadow

        the most patient wave

your shadow is proof

        you have a body

that glows

        the wind flings

up your hair

  like thunder returning

to the sky

  the sky too can be

a homeland to garden

   your hurts in

homeland a word

   for what does

not fail you

  I know you've failed

I know you're failing

better I know

   what you mean

when you say

   I'm sorry

& yes I am

  so proud of you

Acknowledgments

Thank you to the following publications, where versions of these poems first appeared, at times with different names:

Barrelhouse: "An Abridged History"
Blue Mesa Review: "Coping Mechanisms," with thanks to Jake Skeets
BOAAT: "Can You Speak English?"
Carte Blanche: "Frequent Flyer Program"
Cosmonauts Avenue: "When I Say I Want to Learn Your Mother's Recipe, I Mean"
LooseLeaf Magazine: "Immigrant Aubade"
The Margins (Asian American Writers' Workshop): "Phoning Home to Tell My Grandmother I Survived a Hate Crime"; "Sayang"
Ninth Letter: "When My Grandmother Begins to Forget"
Passages North: "Interruption: B-Side"
PRISM *international:* "In Defence of My Roommate's Dog," with thanks to Ariana Brown
The Quarry (Split This Rock): "Self-Portrait as Pop Culture Reference"
THIS *Magazine:* "Bordersong"
Vagabond City Lit: "Birthright"

All my gratitude to the editors and writers who have guided me in evolving this manuscript: Hanif Abdurraqib, Eduardo C. Corral, Jake Skeets, syan jay, Jody Chan, and, of course, my dear and transcendent friend and editor, Jasmine Gui.

Confetti poppers and champagne flutes of thank-yous to the team at Arsenal Pulp Press, especially Brian Lam and Jazmin Welch, for believing in my work, and for their infinite trust in allowing this manuscript to evolve into its current form. A hundred thousand thank-yous to Mia for the beautiful cover and their endless patience in the process.

To the great loves whose tenderness have been a balm for all my days, thank you: Abby Ho, syan jay, Beni Xiao, Nuramelina Amin, Anisa Noor, Allyson Aritcheta, Kiraneet Bains, Andrea Lacson, Jyo, Sarah Quinto, Jennifer Su, Erin Kong, Elise Yoon, and everyone at the Project 40 Collective.

To the creative powerhouses whom I am lucky enough to call friends, what a miracle it is to create alongside each other in this era. Thank you: Whitney French, Laetitia Keok, Brandon Wint, Aseja Dava, Nshira Turkson, Yves Olade, Kai Cheng Thom, Alicia Elliott, L Akhter, Eli Tareq El Bechelany-Lynch, Rebecca Salazar Leon, Cason Sharpe, Nisha Patel, Christina Im, Erin Jin Mei O'Malley, Jade Zhang, Wenting Li, Ryookyung Kim, and future friends I have yet to meet.

To the tremendous lights whose work and presence have illuminated my days, thank you: Ocean Vuong, Hieu Minh Nguyen, Yanyi, Canisia Lubrin, Franny Choi, Vivek Shraya, Vanessa Angélica Villarreal, Billy-Ray Belcourt, Rajiv Mohabir, Jen Sookfong Lee, and countless others.

To Honeybee, although you are a dog and cannot read: thank you for reminding me we deserve love simply because we are here.

Notes

"Rina Sawayama Sings 'I Wanna Be Where You Are'" borrows lines from Rina Sawayama's "Where U Are."

"Field Notes: Time Travel" borrows its form from Layli Long Soldier's "Obligations 2" and is after Richard Siken's "Visible World."

"In My Next Life as a Fruit Tree" is after Hala Alyan's "Spoiler."

"In the Mood for Love" borrows its title from Wong Kar-Wai's film *In the Mood for Love.*

"Self-Portrait as Pop Culture Reference" borrows and alters language from Ocean Vuong's "To My Father / To My Future Son."

"Instructions for a Transmutation Circle" is after Raveena's "If Only."

"Immigrant Aubade" is after Rajiv Mohabir's "Immigrant Aria." It is written for Jasmine and Abby.

"Interruption: B-Side" borrows its form from Hala Alyan's "Interactive :: House Saints," Doyali Islam's "Cat and Door," and Rita Dove's "Mirror."

"Someone in Some Future Time" borrows its title from Sappho's "You May Forget But."

"Listen I Love You Joy Is Coming" borrows its title from Kim Addonizio's "To the Woman Crying Uncontrollably in the Next Stall."

"I Always Bet on Losing Dogs" borrows its title from Mitski's song of the same name.

"En Route to the Sixth Station, Chihiro Counts the Clouds" is after Hanif Abdurraqib's "Carly Rae Jepsen — E•MO•TION."

"That Time I Thought Phoebe Bridgers Sang, 'When I Grow Up, I'm Gonna Look Up from My Phone and See My Wife'" borrows lines from Phoebe Bridgers' "Garden Song."

"I Am My Dreaming Self Getting Better at This" borrows its title from Sarah Gambito's "Shrewd and Beautiful Is My New York," and borrows its form from Eduardo C. Corral's "Velvet Mesquite." It is written after Ocean Vuong's "Eurydice."

Photo credit: May Truong Photography

Natalie Wee is a queer creator. In addition to *Beast at Every Threshold*, she is the author of *Our Bodies and Other Fine Machines* (special edition, San Press, 2021). Her work was named first runner-up for the 2020 Pacific Spirit Poetry Prize, winner of the 2019 *Blue Mesa Review* Summer Contest for poetry, and a Best of the Net finalist. Born in Singapore to Malaysian parents, Natalie is currently a settler in Tkaronto and was part of Project 40 Collective, a Tkaronto-based pan-Asian artist community. She currently edits for Climate Justice Toronto and offers free editorial services for writers of colour. Learn more at *natalieweewrites.com*.